THE NATIONAL TRUST

THE FIRE AT UPPARK

ADAM NICOLSON

Acknowledgments

This account of the fire at Uppark could not have been written without a great deal of time and help from many people. They include: Fred Aldsworth; Catherine Bennett; Brian Bloomfield; Martin Drury; Daryl Fowler; Mary Goodwin; John Hart; Gervase Jackson-Stops; Helen Lloyd; Brian Mallory; Christine Marshall; Jane Mathews; members of the Meade-Fetherstonhaugh family; Sheila Mortimer; Peter Pearce; Alison Prebble; Julian Prideaux; Hugh Routh; Mary Scott; David Sekers; Rachel Thackray and Peter Thuring. Particular thanks are due to Christopher Rowell, the Trust's Historic Buildings Representative for the Southern Region, who has been of immense assistance throughout. In London the production of this booklet has been overseen with unfailing courtesy, efficiency and charm by Margaret Willes and Samantha Wyndham. Many thanks to them all.

Picture Credits

The National Trust Photographic Library: cover (Ian West), pp.1 (John Bethell),4 (John Bethell), 7 (J.Pipkin), 8 (D.M. Nicholson), 9 (J. Whitaker), 10 (John Bethell), 11 (A.Pressi), 19 (D.J. Coke), 30-31 (Ian West), 34-35 (Ian West), 38 (Tim Stephens), 39 top (Patsy Fagan), 39 bottom left, 39 bottom right (Tim Stephens), 40 top (Patsy Fagan), 40 centre and bottom (David Bradfield), 41 (David Bradfield), 42 (Ian West), 43 (David Bradfield), 44 top left (David Bradfield), 44 top right (David Bradfield), 44 bottom left (Patsy Fagan), 44 bottom right (David Bradfield), 46, 47 (Patsy Fagan), 48 (John Bethell); Sheila Atkinson: pp.12, 15 (all); by courtesy of The News, Portsmouth: pp. 20, 22, 23, 24, 26, 28, 32, 36; by courtesy of TVS, Southampton: 27 (all), 28.

Designed, edited and produced by Toucan Books Limited, London.

ISBN 07078 0124 9

PREFACE

The fire at Uppark was one of the greatest tragedies for the National Trust. All of us, whether members, volunteers, staff, family, local people or visitors from all over the world, feel bereaved.

When we took the decision that Uppark should be restored, we realised it would take several years, and would require painstaking recording, as well a great variety of conservation skills. We undertook to record all the stages of the work, and acknowledged that our public would want to learn about the whole restoration project from the outset.

When the project is finished, we hope that a full visual record, and at least one publication will be produced. But that will be several years into the future; the immediate need is to put on record the tragedy that occurred in August 1989.

This publication can therefore be regarded as the first chapter of a much longer book.

Angus Stirling

DIRECTOR - GENERAL

All proceeds from this publication will go towards a fund for the purchase of items for Uppark House

THE HOUSE

UPPARK WAS PERFECT. It was a place of stilled richness, complete in itself, enshrining just over a century of the best of English taste, from about 1690, when the house was built, to about 1815, when it entered a sort of embalming sleep. Throughout all the tides of Victorian, Edwardian and twentieth-century fashion, almost nothing changed at Uppark. It was kept as it was, glamorous but the glamour fading, curtains and bed-hangings repaired not replaced, paintings and pierglasses remaining where the people who had first bought them had hung them, wallpapers faded but unstripped, gilt unregilded, tables and chairs unaltered, vases, carpets, sofas, bookcases, candlesticks, sconces and clocks -- all this untouched and unmoved. The house was filled with a thick and tangible quiet. Everything at Uppark was right, 'as if,' in the words of Nigel Nicolson, written more than twenty years ago, 'all civilisation had led up to this point in space and time, and there was no object in going further.'

Uppark is -- one should continue to use the present tense -- in one of the most beautiful situations in England. It stands four-square, high on the crest of the Sussex Downs, open to the sun and the view, looking out southwards over the generous folds and hollows of the chalk, as though on the highest balcony of a broad and sloping theatre, to the distant waters of Spithead beyond them. There is no garden on this side; the Downs run up to the walls of the house. The southern light floods into the sun-bleached rooms.

The east front of Uppark, perhaps designed by William Talman in about 1690.

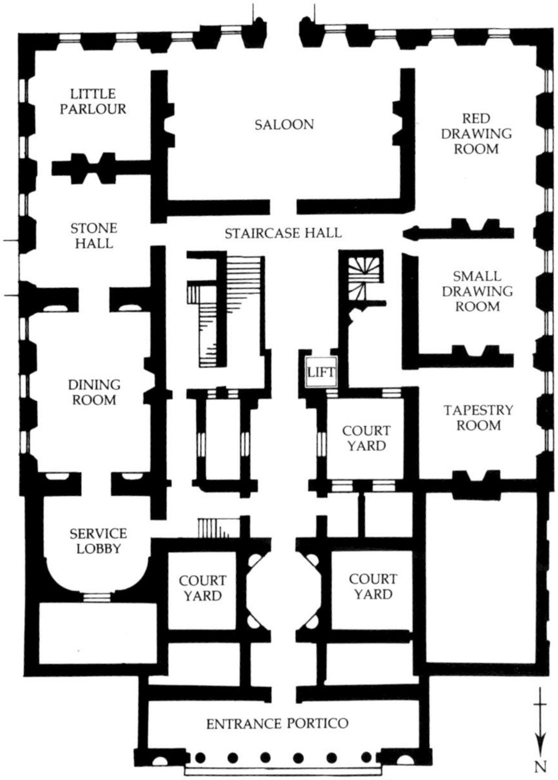

Ground floor plan

There may have been a house here since the sixteenth century, but in about 1690 the history of Uppark began again. An odious man built a beautiful house. Forde, Lord Grey of Werke, had led a long and successful career of double-dealing, political opportunism, craven submission and frank betrayal which eventually brought him the Earldom of Tankerville and his appointment under William III to the office of Lord Privy Seal. This man is the first of the three great creators of Uppark.

The house he built, probably after William of Orange had arrived on the English throne, might be seen as yet another piece of flattery. It is Dutch in inspiration, perhaps designed by William Talman, one of the architects of Chatsworth. The basic structure is simple, almost toy-like: two brick storeys raised on a low basement are surmounted by a steeply pitched roof in which there is an attic. A pediment is set over the middle of the south front, festooned with swags of stone flowers and a coat of arms, and a deep, heavily carved modillion cornice runs around the whole building. There is nothing flashy; it is strict and rich. 'The general effect,' as one of the owners of Uppark wrote, 'is one of gravity and repose, of seemliness and order. It is an architecture that neither deceives nor declaims; its virtue lies in its grace and calculated simplicity.'

In 1746 Matthew Fetherstonhaugh, the young Northumberland cousin of a childless Essex millionaire, found himself the unexpected beneficiary of a vast inheritance, whose only conditions were that he got himself a baronetcy and came to live in the south. He bought Uppark; he became Sir Matthew; he married Sarah Lethieullier, a woman as vital, as hungry for new things and new adventures as himself. With her he toured the Continent collecting wonderful pictures -- Batonis, Canalettos, Giordanos, Zuccarellis, often in sets of four or six -- and masses of silver, gold-anchor Chelsea porcelain, carpets and mahogany furniture, all of the most fashionable European kind. They ordered tables from Florence, chinoiserie commodes in the French taste, giltwood rococo pierglasses and it all came in packing-cases to Sussex.

Detail of one of the rococo giltwood pierglasses in the Red Drawing Room, brought to Uppark by Sir Matthew Fetherstonhaugh in about 1755. It was rescued in the middle of the night during the fire.

Uppark itself was reshaped to house these extraordinary treasures. Not every room was redecorated -- the Stone Hall and the apartments on the first floor were probably left much as Lord Tankerville had had them -- but elsewhere panelling was removed and new flock wallpapers were put up on the walls. Bottle-green silk and crimson damasks covered the chairs. In many of the rooms elegant rococo and, later, neo-classical plaster ceilings were installed. The crowning achievement of this second great phase at Uppark was the Saloon, a double-cube along the south front of the house, a long, pale room where in the doorways, the reveals of the windows, the picture-surrounds

Left: The Saloon, Uppark's most beautiful room, created by Sir Matthew and redecorated, probably by Humphry Repton, in the early nineteenth century.

Right: A capital and part of the entablature from a doorcase in the Saloon.

and above all in the coves and panels of the astonishing plaster ceiling, the most delicate of flowers and tendrils played over the surfaces behind them. This ceiling, like the others, is at the moment in pieces, carefully preserved in a series of plastic bread trays.

In 1774 Sir Matthew died. His son Harry was twenty and set for a wild time. For about thirty-five years Sir Harry gave enormous parties, gambled, raced horses and, with exquisite, Francophile taste, bought almost as many beautiful objects as his father had done, adding masses of French furniture and Sèvres porcelain to the Uppark ensemble. Most glamorously of all, for just over a year, Sir Harry loved Emma Hart, a London nightclub hostess of quite disabling beauty. She was later, as Emma Hamilton, to become Nelson's mistress and she may, in the most famous of Uppark stories, have danced naked here on the dining room table. One can only hope that the story is true.

The Prince of Wales often came to stay at Uppark for parties which were generally acknowledged to be the best in England. But in about 1810 Sir Harry quarrelled with the Prince -- the cause of the row is unknown -- and Sir Harry withdrew from society. The third reshaping layer was now added to Uppark, as Sir Harry formed a friendship with Humphry Repton, the great landscape designer.

Repton added a portico to the north front, made changes inside the house, probably overseeing the repainting and gilding of the Saloon, and built a tunnel connecting the house to the old kitchen, in a separate building to the north-east. This was the tunnel by which the visitors were evacuated on the day of the fire.

There was one last adventure for Sir Harry. When he was seventy-one he married his dairy-maid, Mary Ann Bullock, who was twenty. He had heard her singing in the little tiled dairy which Repton had designed for him next to the stable block. Sir Harry lived until 1846, Mary Ann until 1874 and her sister Frances, who had come to live with them, until 1895. It was this longevity, this direct link between 1774, when Sir Harry had inherited the house, and 1895, when Frances finally passed it on to her adopted heir, which guaranteed the survival of Uppark. In the late nineteenth century the house was occupied by a pair of old ladies in black velvet -- Frances Bullock and her companion Miss Sutherland, said to have been Sir Harry's natural child. Together they led quiet, shrunken lives, spending days on end talking about the weather and stroking their pet dogs in the Little Parlour. At a time when H.G.Wells's mother became the housekeeper downstairs, stillness had arrived at Uppark. The old ladies were custodians of Sir Harry's memory, conserving by doing almost nothing, as if Uppark was not theirs to Victorianise. It was theirs to look after, not theirs to change.

That principle has remained true in this century. The owners of Uppark,

Sir Harry Fetherstonhaugh, connoisseur, gambler and lover of Emma Hart, in a portrait by Benjamin West.

The state bed in the Tapestry Room.

first Colonel Turnour-Fetherstonhaugh, then, in 1931, Admiral Sir Herbert Meade-Fetherstonhaugh and his son Richard, and later the National Trust, to whom they gave the house in 1954, have all seen it as a place too precious to alter.

In this way, and half by accident, Uppark became one of the earliest places where conservation of the whole house, its every constituent part, was seen as the governing idea. Lady Meade-Fetherstonhaugh pioneered the techniques of textile conservation here in the 1930s; in the 1950s, at a time when, for example, repainting of woodwork was the norm, the Trust made it a principle to conserve the original paint. Uppark was not simply a building with objects. It was an organic, connected whole, a layered, rich and complicated thing, in which lessening of any part would be a lessening of the whole. That is one reason for the sadness over the fire; it was not a museum at which the fire occurred, but a house and the home of a family.

THE FIRE

ABOUT 32,000 people a year visit Uppark. By mid-afternoon on 30 August 1989 there had already been about 270 visitors to the house. Many of them were now in the National Trust shop in the basement, buying souvenirs before moving on to tea in the Old Kitchen. It was a beautifully sunny day, with a bright blue sky, and members of the Meade-Fetherstonhaugh family, including Harriet Cossart, Emma Goad and several children, were enjoying the afternoon around the swimming pool. The day was not particularly warm. A strong breeze was blowing in from the south-west, as it often does on the Downs.

The year before, after the regular five-yearly examination by the Trust's architect, the decision had been taken to replace the lead on the roof. It had last been renewed in the 1930s and was beginning to perish. For a year the scaffolding had encased the house, as the builders worked their way around the roof, replacing the lead flashings at the foot of the chimneys and relining the gutters above the deep modillion cornice. The builders had reached the last part of the job, the lead covering on the eastern side of the pediment on the south front. They were due to finish the following day. That afternoon, as on so many before it, they were welding together some sheets of lead.

Visitors evacuated from the house watch the progress of the fire from the west lawn. This photograph by a member of the public was taken at about 4.15pm on 30 August 1989.

At 3.38 the fire alarm went off in the house. It is automatically linked to the fire stations at Petersfield (six miles away) and Midhurst (nine miles) and to the headquarters of the West Sussex Fire Service in Chichester, about twelve miles from

Uppark. Brian Bloomfield, the National Trust's administrator for the last four years at Uppark, knew what to do. He had just taken up his position at the ticket kiosk by the Golden Gates, the entrance to the house and garden, so that the other members of staff could have some tea. When he heard the alarm-bell he tried to telephone down to the house to check that it *was* the alarm bell he was hearing but could get no answer. He then shut up the kiosk, opened the Golden Gates wide so that the fire engines could drive right up to Repton's portico on the north front, summoned the car park attendant and told him to keep the driveway clear and all the members of the public out. This was normal routine.

His wife Joan was working in the basement shop, which was full of people. She and the National Trust room stewards cleared everyone out of the house, quite calmly, without any panic, directing them out on to the lawns, through the portico on the north front and along Repton's underground passageway leading to the Old Kitchen, now a tea-room. Many of them thought it was simply a fire-practice. Jan Smith, the wife of the custodian Brian Smith, was working there when she got the news. She rushed to join forces with Joan Bloomfield. The Smiths lived in the attic flat of the main house.

Opposite: A sequence of photographs, taken by a visitor to the house, chart the first moments of the fire: at about 3.45pm, workmen, who had been repairing the roof, are on the scaffolding; flames and smoke appear from the pediment and then spread through the roof void to the south-eastern corner of the house, taking serious hold. At about 4 o'clock, the first firemen reach the top scaffolding and with the water from their hose dampen the flames, producing a plume of smoke and steam.

A puff of smoke, a clean white cloudlet of smoke, had appeared on the eastern side of the pediment. Workmen from the building firm attempted to put the fire out with a pair of fire extinguishers but they had no effect. One or two visitors were on the lawn taking photographs of these first moments of the fire. Meanwhile on the ground floor Jan Smith and Joan Bloomfield were starting to clear the moveables out of the Little Parlour, the room at the south-east corner of the house immediately below the seat of the fire two storeys above.

About a quarter of an hour had passed since the alarms had first sounded when the first fire engine -- it was the Petersfield team -- came up the long and woody drive to Uppark. They could see smoke coming from the roof and, while still

on the move, radioed for two more fire engines. Midhurst arrived a minute or two afterwards, reported flames and requested a further two appliances. Nine minutes later another two were requested, two minutes after that another four, and quarter an hour after that another six. Half an hour after the fire brigade had first arrived there were four fire engines at the house and another sixteen on their way. Eventually 27 fire engines and 156 firemen would attend the fire, coming from the West Sussex, Hampshire and Surrey Brigades.

One team of firemen went up on to the top scaffolding to get some water jets to play on the parts of the south front that were visibly burning. But roof fires can only be properly fought from the inside and Bloomfield led another team up the inside staircase to the attic corridor. The firemen managed for a moment to get to an opening into the roof space but the fire was already too fierce and they were beaten back. As they retreated in front of the fire, the ceiling of that corridor collapsed on top of them in a mass of burning attic timbers. None of the firemen was seriously hurt, but throughout the fire many of them were to suffer small and painful burns from the drops of molten lead pouring off the roof. It was obvious that the attic flat was no longer safe and the firemen withdrew from it, back down to the first floor. On their way down they took one thing with them: an oil painting of a dog, all that was to survive from either the first or the attic floors.

It is a measure of the attention to detail involved in the care of Uppark that the Bloomfields and perhaps in particular the Smiths, whose every possession was now under dire threat, worried instead about the damage that might be done to the treasures of the house by the water from the firemen's hoses. As the first move of many that afternoon to prevent water damage, Brian Bloomfield collected a bucket and a couple of plastic dustbins from the kitchen on the first floor and put them under the hose to prevent a carpet belonging to the Meade-Fetherstonhaugh family from getting wet. He, Brian Smith and a team of about six male stewards then cleared everything they could move -- paintings, china, the furniture that was not too heavy to lift -- from the family's drawing room, immediately below the fire in the south-east corner of the house. When they had finished in the room, leaving it virtually cleared, they could see a row of water drops coming through the ceiling from the deluge which the fire brigade was now pouring into the attic floor above.

No one had yet realised that the fire would be total and these precious objects were not taken downstairs but moved simply to another first floor room on the west side of the house. They, like all the other family possessions on the first floor at Uppark, have now been totally destroyed.

From the beginning, members of the family had been deeply involved in the removal of books, paintings and furniture from the house. Meanwhile, on the ground floor Joan Bloomfield and Jan Smith, having systematically cleared the Little Parlour, began to move into other rooms. Joan Bloomfield gathered a team of eight stewards and took them into the Saloon, where anything moveable was taken out -- small pieces of furniture, a couple of small cupboards, a fine set of Georgian giltwood armchairs with tapestry seats and backs. After Emma Goad had told the firemen about them, three French tapestries from the State Bedroom, attached to the wall with velcro, were easily pulled down and away. All these objects were piled up in the Repton portico at the northern entrance to the house.

Harriet Cossart and Emma Goad were supervising the removal of the first of the contents to the tea room and then, as it filled up, to the stables, where John West, the carpenter, removed a window so that the objects could be passed through to shelter. The attic and roof were now totally ablaze. A high tail of smoke, brown and black at its roots, coloured with the dark bubbles and blades of flame, streamed away from the house like a beacon, a high white diagonal blown north-eastwards across Sussex by the wind. Many in the surrounding villages thought it was a stubble fire out of control.

Inside the house a critical moment had been reached. The first floor ceilings were in danger. In one or two places they had already broken through and the fire was showing in the first floor windows. Just as Harriet Cossart was trying to get upstairs to her family flat on the first floor, the firemen ordered everyone out of the house. The team of stewards who had been clearing the drawing-room in the south-east corner were sent downstairs and the first floor was given over to the fire. Only the prints and wallpaper from the Print Room, one of the five or six most perfect examples in the country, were saved. By good fortune almost the entire decorative scheme for this room had been removed for restoration and was in London awaiting reinstatement. The rest, the mirror from the Print Room, still there in a packing case ready for removal, the bleached white oak floors, never polished, the faded chintzes and eighteenth-century textiles, the seventeenth-century panelling, the rooms with their incomparable views out over the green and yellow landscape of the late English summer -- all this was burnt.

Kenneth Lloyd, Deputy Chief Fire Officer for West Sussex, had arrived at the house at about 4.25. The large white hydraulic platform, a jointed crane from which firemen could shoot water into the heart of the fire, had followed him up the drive. It was to dominate the scene for the rest of the afternoon and the night. Water was starting to be a problem. The firemen had already exhausted the four hundred gallons in each fire engine and were now drawing on the underground water tank beneath the Dairy. Lloyd recognised very early on that this was a major fire and that the water tanks at Uppark itself would not be enough. In an operation extraordinary for its rational calm in crisis, Lloyd continued to keep water coming on to the fire for all except three brief moments during the afternoon and night. First the Dairy tank was exhausted, then the Uppark swimming pool, each of these sources just overlapping into the next. But they were not enough. Lloyd radioed for five more fire engines and a hose-layer. When they arrived a hose was laid from the

At about 4.30 the hydraulic platform from Chichester arrived at the fire and began pouring water into the northern parts of the house. By then the attic was gone and the fire was beginning to break through into the first floor.

main in South Harting, well over a mile away, all the way up the hill to the house, with five fire engines parked at intervals along it, pumping the water to the fire. But within a few minutes the South Harting main collapsed, unable to take the demands being made on it. Water failed for a short time to reach the house, where firemen on the scaffold, finding their hoses dry, bellowed down for more.

Lloyd's only alternative was to set up a shuttle to a five-inch main a few miles away. From about five o'clock onwards, and throughout the night, six fire engines and two 5,000 gallon water carriers drove to and fro between the house and the main, debouching their water into holding tanks near the Golden Gates before returning for more. But this was not enough either and Lloyd's men managed to find a private lake, recently stocked with fish, near South Harting. No fire engines could reach it -- the lake was on the far side of a wood -- but they put in a string of portable pumps and hoses which were then tapped into the main relay up the road. By the morning the lake was sucked nearly dry. The hundreds of fish were thick and

Fire teams on the gravel at the north front of the house.

visible in the little water that remained in the lake. Another private tank up on the hill itself was found and the relay was finally switched to there. This persistent effort and ingenuity in getting water to Uppark, a high and naturally dry place, 350 feet above the springline at South Harting, says a great deal for the skill and expertise of the fire service in very difficult circumstances.

But the water-search was only a third of the brigade's job: there was the fire itself to think about and the salvage of the contents on the ground floor. By about five o'clock, the fire was well established on the first floor, reaching it both through the collapse of ceilings above and more insidiously down the narrow gap between the brick or masonry of the walls themselves and the panelling or plaster facings of the rooms inside. One can imagine this, a thin skin of fire, wrapped all the way around the house and then bursting inwards, into the rooms themselves, where it reached a wooden door or lintel. All is destroyed on the first floor now, but on the ground floor, where much more has survived, the evidence is still there: a wooden lintel, utterly charred and blackened, and all around it the intricacies of eighteenth-century moulded and gilded plaster still complete, virtually untouched.

The Staircase Hall was now a mass of sparks and falling timber. Under cover of spray jets from the doorway, fire crews went in to save the paintings, some very large seventeenth-century views of Uppark by Tillemans, six foot by ten foot each, and a series of mid-eighteenth century family portraits by Arthur Devis, the painted history of the house and its family. With the sparks and timbers falling on top of them, the fire crews wrenched these paintings off the wall, levering them off with crowbars and then wobbling them out through the doorways into the open air. The gun cupboard at the foot of the stairs was cleared after Charlie Cossart had warned the firemen of the danger.

A few minutes later the staircase crashed through and was engulfed. This was the beginning of the firemen's salvage operation, which lasted, in this first phase, until about six. Everything that could move was moved. The fire crews as they arrived at the north front were told to put on their breathing sets and then instructed on where to go, what to save. Each crew, an officer and four or five men, went in as a group and out as a group, to minimise the chances of a man becoming trapped. On each occasion the officer watched for collapse of the structure while the men gathered up as much as they could carry.

At about 5 o'clock the porcelain from the basement is handed out along a chain of rescue workers. The fire is well established in the first floor rooms.

The contents of Uppark, some of them for the first time in 250 years, started to move out of the house and on to the lawns, and from there into the Stables and the Old Kitchen. Emma Goad, who remembered her grandmother showing her as a girl the exquisite eighteenth-century doll's house, personally instructed the firemen on how to remove it. The huge early Wilton carpet in the Saloon -- it needed eight men to carry it -- was rolled up and dragged out on to the south lawn where National Trust stewards pulled it further away. Members of the Meade-Fetherstonhaugh family formed the chains of firemen, stewards and visitors to pass out stacks of Meissen and Chelsea plates from the basement, each plate worth many thousands of pounds. The stewards' training had told them to carry only one piece of porcelain at a time. That was not possible now and the porcelain came out in clutched-at bundles. The very best Meissen coffee service was carried out in a hip bath from the butler's pantry. Incredibly, out of sixty crates of porcelain that were brought out of the ground floor and basement, only three pieces were in any way damaged during the whole course of the fire: a handle off a tureen, some chips out of a saucer, and a recurrence of an old break in another piece where the glue failed. The priceless Giordanos, Batonis and Zuccarellis, along with all the other pictures, were taken out and laid face down on the lawn. The high wind made it difficult to manhandle the larger pictures, but it is one of the great blessings that there was no rain that afternoon.

Kenneth Lloyd through a megaphone directed the firemen still on the scaffolding above him. The boards on the scaffolding themselves started to burn around the firemen's feet and other crews sprayed them from below. A gilt rococo mirror lay face-up on the grass and newsmen filmed the smoky sky reflected in it. The diesel engines of the firemen's pumps moaned and whined in the background. The house was surrounded by a slithering tangle of red hoses. From time to time, as a major beam collapsed in a shower of sparks, a heavy thumping shudder could be felt up through the feet on the lawn. Resting firemen packed themselves into National Trust benches, four to a bench. Meanwhile the house spat and crackled, the sound of a bonfire, the smell, simply, of wood burning.

The salvage well underway: books, pictures and furniture from the Saloon are taken out on to the south lawn, ready for removal to the Stables and the Old Kitchen.

One of the giltwood side-tables from the Saloon, its marble top already removed, is taken to safety down the Saloon door steps. This table was probably one of Sir Matthew's first purchases, made in about 1740.

At National Trust Head Office in London and at Regional Headquarters, in Polesden Lacey near Dorking, all the Trust's conservation resources were being mobilised. Experts from all over the country in textiles, paintings, furniture, decorative metalwork, gilded wood, wallpapers, plaster, stone and marble were being telephoned at work or home, wherever they could be found, and told to go to Uppark. A van containing emergency equipment - sheets of industrial polythene, rolls of blotting paper and bubble-wrap, hard hats, torches, walkie-talkies, brushes, screwdrivers and miniature hoovers - was summoned from Kingston Lacy in Dorset. In London, National Trust secretaries were sent out to a late-night Sainsbury's to buy up all the absorbent materials they could find. Key-holders for branches of W.H. Smith's were sought through the police, so the shops could be opened and supplies of blotting paper brought to Uppark. The switchboards in London and Polesden Lacey were besieged by the press. One journalist refused to get off the line until he had his story.

By about six o'clock that evening, the fire had reached a sort of plateau. Everything that was easily moved was now out on the lawns or already transferred to the shelter of the outbuildings. The fire itself had stabilised and the huge tower of smoke, which had dominated the landscape for miles around earlier in the afternoon, had now shrunk away.

The roof had gone entirely and there in the attic the internal walls and chimney stacks stood up above the level of the cornice like the funnels of a quietly burning liner. One or two fires were still visible on the first floor, but among those watching from the lawns some hope flickered that this would be the end of it. Maybe the fire would be stopped here and the state rooms on the ground floor would remain untouched.

Senior members of the National Trust staff had now begun to arrive: Martin Drury, the Historic Buildings Secretary, David Sekers, the Regional Director, Peter

Fire dominates the first floor, while firemen inside the Red Drawing Room below it retrieve objects according to the guidance of National Trust stewards, who are standing on the lawn outside.

Uppark burning. Stills from a helicopter-shot news-video, overflying the house at about 5.15pm. The high tail of smoke was visible for miles around. Many thought it was a stubble fire out of control. The hydraulic platform has moved round to the east of the house; the attic floor has gone; and most of the contents of the Saloon are already out on the south lawn.

Pearce, the Managing Agent for the property and Christopher Rowell, the Historic Buildings Representative for the Southern Region. Many of them had been involved with the Trust's re-evaluation of their emergency procedures in the light of the fire at Hampton Court three years before. As a result of what they had learnt and thought about, it was clear, despite everything that had already been done, that a great deal more, in the way of curtains, wallpapers, pierglasses and heavy pieces of furniture, should be removed from the house if that was in any way possible. These things

Approaching 6 o'clock the fire has stabilised in all but the north-east corner of the house where the hydraulic platform is tackling the flames. Peter Pearce, the Managing Agent for Uppark, comforts Harriet Cossart, the eldest daughter of Jean and the late Richard Meade-Fetherstonhaugh, whose home has been destroyed.

were crucial to the character of Uppark, and were anyway valuable in themselves, and their loss would be a disaster.

Soon after 6.30 the fire began its second phase. Sparks started to fall in through the ceiling of the Stone Hall on the ground floor. Martin Drury experienced the most frustrating of moments. There in the Stone Hall, only ten yards away from where he was standing, were a pair of rare and valuable *scagliola* tables which Sir Matthew had ordered from Florence in the 1750s. Could the firemen rescue them now before it was too late? No, the ceiling was on the point of collapse and it would be too dangerous. A few minutes later the collapse occurred and the hall was filled with flames. Amazingly, one of these tables survives, its top broken in half but mendable. A falling beam landed directly on the other and it was smashed into many pieces. It is nevertheless possible that this table too will be repaired.

Elsewhere, particularly in the south-west corner of the house, events were more encouraging. As the night came on, Christopher Rowell, accompanied by a team of firemen, toured the outside of the house, requesting eighteenth-century silk brocade curtains here, huge lengths of flock wallpapers there. They were torn down by the firemen and thrown out on to the lawn. Helpers transferred them to the Dairy where conservators would find them later that night. Early the next morning, one of the great curtains from the Saloon was found in a crumpled, wet heap where the firemen had tossed it. Three huge rococo mirrors in the Red and Small Drawing Rooms were still fixed to the wall. Drury and Rowell asked the firemen if they could rescue them. One of the firemen started to break the window glass with his axe. 'Actually,' Drury said, hesitating, 'that is *eighteenth*-century glass. The windows do throw up easily enough.' The firemen pushed up the windows and under a sprayed arch of water from two hoses, to catch and cool the falling embers, they went in. 'How are the mirrors fixed?' they shouted from the inside. 'Two screws at the top, two at the bottom.' 'We haven't got a screwdriver.' A screwdriver was found from

Soon after 6.30, the fire begins its second phase, breaking through to the ground floor in the Stone Hall.

DENNIS

the Kingston Lacy van, the mirrors were released and one by one handed out through the windows, the heat-smashed mirror-glass falling from the frames as they were passed out. The gilded, liquid curves of the frames of two of them were not seriously damaged. The other was smoking, the giltwood charred.

At the instigation of Jean Meade-Fetherstonhaugh, who had arrived from London, silver was rescued by Brian Bloomfield from the safe in the basement, now a foot deep in water. On the floor above, doors, sections of panelling, dado rails and the gilded fillets which fixed the sections of wallpaper to the wall were being removed for safekeeping. Soon after midnight, painting conservators arrived and began to tend to the pictures.

At about 2.30 in the morning, for the first time since early in the afternoon, National Trust staff were allowed into the building. Kenneth Lloyd guided Drury and Rowell into the northern, Repton end of the house where the ceilings had not yet collapsed.

They pointed out to him anything that might be removed later in the night. The empty rooms were in a state of suspended animation, lit by the flames, a ghostly version of that final look around a house from which the removal men have taken everything and which the owners are about to leave for the last time.

Outside again, Drury and Rowell made their final requests. In the Dining Room where Emma Hart had dined and maybe danced, a beautiful overmantel mirror remained above the fireplace. A fireman was sent in to get it. The mirror, with its original, subtly coloured eighteenth-century glass, was too much for him. 'Do you want the glass?' the fireman shouted. Normally, to move this precious object would have been a long, slow and careful operation. 'Never mind the glass,' Drury shouted in, the fireman swung at it it with his axe, the mirror-glass fell in shards to the floor and the frame alone was carried out of the building to safety.

Standing outside the Little Parlour, where the old ladies had sat for so many months and years, a fireman was hosing flames that had broken out in the top corner of the room. The chandelier was still there in the empty room swinging to and fro in the heat and smoke. The jet of water from the fireman's hose was making it spin like a whirligig. 'Try to avoid the chandelier,' they told him and conscientiously he did what they asked. Later on, at about five o'clock in the morning, the large chimney stack above the Little Parlour collapsed, crashing straight through the ceiling and on into the basement below, carrying the ceiling, floor and chandelier with it.

Opposite page: As the evening darkens, firemen in breathing sets direct their jets through the broken roof into the Staircase Hall, the furnace at the heart of the fire.

Drury and Rowell had one last vision. In the Tapestry Room, the state bed, with a fat little cherub standing at each of its four top corners, traditionally brought to Uppark by Sarah Lethieullier on her marriage to Sir Matthew, was still there and still complete. Most of the ceiling had held, but sparks were falling through it on to the bed. 'That's the last we'll see of that,' Drury and Rowell said to each other, before leaving Uppark at about 3.15 in the morning.

Deep into the night, the fire has reached the ground floor, showing in the windows of the Stone Hall and the Dining Room. The chimney stack above the Little Parlour, at the near south-eastern corner of the house, is visibly notched where it joins the gable. This stack would collapse, at about 5 o'clock in the morning, taking everything below it down into the basement.

THE SAVING OF UPPARK

THE TAPESTRY ROOM ceiling was still there in the morning and the bed was intact, leaning drunkenly, covered in ash and soot, but with the red silk and applied crewel work of the tester and back substantially undamaged. Then, acting under instructions from John Hart and the conservators who look after the furniture at Uppark, the firemen dismantled it, lifting off the top, unbolting the lower sections, and passed it out piece by piece through the window. Twenty minutes later the ceiling fell in a broken chaos of plaster and timber.

A Pompeian tide of wet charcoal sludge covered the ground floor and basement. Here and there small fires continued to burn. In every room charred and fallen timbers lay silently among the blue spiralling smoke. It was a Piranesi scene, floorless perspectives from the basement to the sky, upstairs fireplaces opening on to the void, masonry revealed where the panelling had gone. Large parts of the gilded carving in the Saloon retained every notch and detail that had been given them in the 1760s. Most was untouched, but where a burning joist had fallen against a wall or doorcase, the egg and dart, the flowers and tendrils had been perfectly and exactly transmuted into charcoal.

The morning after. Uppark stands open to the sky; fire engines and their hoses still surround the house; on the west lawn charred timbers lie on the grass where the firemen have laid them.

And this is where Uppark begins again. It was a day of discovery and relief. In the Saloon most of the carved and gilded doorcases, dado rails and skirting board, the two marble chimneypieces by Thomas Carter, most of the beautiful bleached oak floorboards and Humphry Repton's grey and gold bookcases were all there.

Ash and other debris lie on the mantelshelf of the fireplace in the Saloon. The fireplace itself and the plaster picture-surround above it are virtually undamaged.

The paintings that had been removed the afternoon before could all have gone straight back into the plasterwork panels that had been designed for them. The seventeenth-century panelling in the Dining Room had virtually gone, but in the other rooms many details survived. One thing was clear: Uppark had not been totally gutted.

There is one aspect of the fire which, ironically, had done more to save Uppark than any other. The Staircase Hall had been the wide, roaring chimney at the heart of the fire. Draughts had been sucked in through the outer rooms to feed its great inner furnace. As a result no flames had emerged through the windows to burn the outer face of the building. The skin of Uppark, its subtly lichened and patinated walls, had not been damaged by fire. Apart from the line of spatter-marks, where molten lead from the roof had fallen and then bounced off the scaffolding boards, the outside of Uppark would look again as beautiful, as unhurt, as it had before.

There was much to be done. This was a crisis on a scale never before faced by the Trust. Peter Pearce, the Managing Agent for the property, was confronted with a tangled web of urgency. He arranged emergency housing for the Smiths, who had

Above: Beams and sodden ash from the floors above lie in the remains of the Red Drawing Room.

Right: The Dining Room before the fire and after the debris had been cleared from it. The polythene wrappings protect the few pieces of panelling that remain.

no home to go to. The building itself was still partly on fire and in a dangerouly unstable condition as the fabric cooled. There was a bewildering array of materials -- timber, gilded plaster and wood, metal, ceramics, stone, glass, textiles and paintings -- all in need of sudden intensive care. Long meetings were held on site that Thursday, and for many days afterwards, no break for week-ends, to establish the systems by which Uppark would be saved. Most of the conservators alerted the night before had arrived by 8 o'clock in the morning and had set to work. The three paintings specialists who had been tending to water damage all night were relieved by another team who continued the rescue. Textile conservators took the festoon curtains which had been hurled through the windows and interleaved them with sheets of polythene to keep them wet. Rapid drying would have left them brittle and stained. Trevor Proudfoot, the National Trust adviser on sculpture and stone, was halfway through dismantling the fireplace in the Stone Hall, when a falling brick hit a fireman and they all had to withdraw from the building. Only later was the fireplace boxed in and saved.

Fragments of curtain salvaged from the fire (top); a gilt boss from the plaster ceiling in the Saloon (centre); and one of the modillions from the eaves cornice (below) stored under temporary cover on the lawns.

But the building was unstable and in urgent need of scaffolding braces to support the structure. Here was the first

The sea of dustbins into which the burnt and broken fragments taken from the house were stored prior to sorting and sifting.

of the urgent problems: the scaffolding could not go in until the debris and charcoal sludge had been removed. The two had to be done hand in hand and quickly. A grid was established in each of the rooms, so that the source of all the material removed from the house could be precisely identified. Square by square it was dug out and and placed in the 3860 labelled dustbins which filled the lawns and came to symbolise in the press the salvage of the house. Even as the sludge was removed, amazing discoveries were made deep inside it: the Red Drawing Room carpet, part-folded up and almost untouched, but containing the vestiges of a piano that had once stood on its surface; the lustres of the Little Parlour and Red Drawing Room chandeliers, many unbroken; many pieces, some as large as a dining-room table,

The exquisite eighteenth-century Doll's House among the rest of the salvage in the Orangery.

of the plaster ceiling in the Little Drawing Room; a section of the 1690 staircase balustrade; the metal lantern from the Stone Hall, crushed by two floors falling on top of it, but repairable; a silver-gilt eyeglass, the glass broken but the frame intact; one of the cherubs from the state bed, his face split but his body whole.

An extraordinary atmosphere developed. The loyalty of people to Uppark emerged in a sustained burst of serious and gritty enthusiasm. Sandwiches were made by the hundred, vans full of Mars Bars arrived. Twelve- and fourteen-hour days were worked. Here was a disaster and its solution lay in a combination of hard work and expertise which reminded people of the war.

People from the village, the shock-numbed room stewards, teams of conservators, foresters, wardens, staff and their families from the Regional Office,

National Trust Acorn Camp volunteers, archaeologists from English Heritage, engineers, loss adjusters, platoons of women from the WRVS, a team of Royal Military Police from Chichester - at various times over the next weeks and months more than 200 people were working at Uppark. After three days the water and electricity were restored. All the paintings, furniture and sixty crates of porcelain were packed up and sent away to a safe place. The wallpapers were hurried to the conservation team at the Victoria and Albert Museum in London for drying and stabilisation. Even in the early days it appeared as if large sections of the original wallpapers could be rehung. The textiles were stabilised on site, under the supervision of Jane Mathews, the Trust's adviser on textile conservation.

The first scaffolding went up to brace the pediment and chimney stacks; the debris was slowly removed. Wherever people were working, watchers on the

Glass from the Little Parlour chandelier, found among the debris in the basement.